ADVERTISING OVERLOAD

BY DUCHESS HARRIS, JD, PHD
WITH SUE BRADFORD EDWARDS

Core Library

Cover image: It's easy to feel overwhelmed by advertising these days.

An Imprint of Abdo Publishing
abdopublishing.com

abdopublishing.com

Published by Abdo Publishing, a division of ABDO, PO Box 398166, Minneapolis, Minnesota 55439. Copyright © 2018 by Abdo Consulting Group, Inc. International copyrights reserved in all countries. No part of this book may be reproduced in any form without written permission from the publisher. Core Library™ is a trademark and logo of Abdo Publishing.

Printed in the United States of America, North Mankato, Minnesota
102017
012018

Cover Photo: Shutterstock Images
Interior Photos: Shutterstock Images, 1, 9 (background), 18, 24 (background); iStockphoto, 4–5, 11, 23, 25, 38–39; Dave Martin/AP Images, 7; Red Line Editorial, 9 (foreground), 24 (foreground); Gail Oskin/AP Images, 12–13, 43; Anna Hoychuk/Shutterstock Images, 14–15; Paramount Pictures/Photofest, 20–21; Andrey Popov/Shutterstock Images, 28–29; Adrian Hancu/iStockphoto, 31; Alex Brandon/AP Images, 34–35

Editor: Patrick Donnelly
Imprint Designer: Maggie Villaume
Series Design Direction: Megan Anderson

Publisher's Cataloging-in-Publication Data

Names: Harris, Duchess, author. | Edwards, Sue Bradford, author.
Title: Advertising overload / by Duchess Harris and Sue Bradford Edwards.
Description: Minneapolis, Minnesota : Abdo Publishing, 2018. | Series: News literacy | Includes online resources and index.
Identifiers: LCCN 2017947122 | ISBN 9781532113871 (lib.bdg.) | ISBN 9781532152757 (ebook)
Subjects: LCSH: Advertising--Juvenile literature. | Marketing--Juvenile literature. | Advertising--History--Juvenile literature. | Mass media and propaganda--Juvenile literature.
Classification: DDC 659.1--dc23
LC record available at https://lccn.loc.gov/2017947122

CONTENTS

ADVERTISING WHERE YOU PLAY

The young gamer glanced at the clock. He had enough time to play his favorite strategy game, so he clicked "Play Now." Now the screen read, "Start Here—Free Download."

His older brother had already told him not to click on it. This wasn't part of the game. It was an advertisement designed to look like a game download. If he clicked it, the ad would pull him out of the game and to another site. Instead, he closed the window.

It's nearly impossible to escape advertising, which is even found in video games.

There were so many ads in the game. Some were in sidebars to the left and right of the screen. These were easier to recognize. They were for a fantasy game that looked very different from his game. He was glad he knew what they were. Clicking them would also take him away from his game.

He preferred the ads on his brother's favorite racing game. They were just like the ads in real racing. Some cars were painted with the names and logos of sponsors. There were also ads on billboards near the start of the race. These ads were just part of the background. He didn't have to worry about clicking on them and leaving

SPONSORSHIPS

Race car drivers and teams seek sponsors to help cover their costs. This money pays for racing fees, for car repairs, and even for new cars. A company that sponsors a racing team gets its name and logo on the car and on the drivers' jumpsuits. These are often long-term agreements. The sponsorship may last months or years. In contrast, an ad on a website may appear for only a brief time.

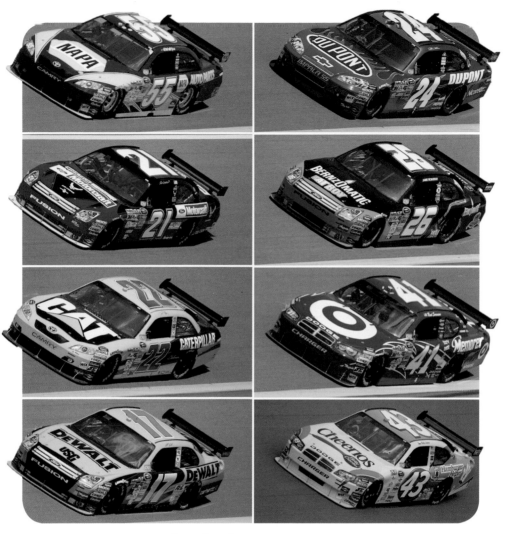

Race cars are covered with advertisements promoting companies that sponsor their teams.

the game. This mattered because he just wanted to play, not to shop. Still, he knew no matter where the ads appeared, they were trying to sell him something.

ADVERTISING

An advertisement, or ad for short, is a way of sharing information. Some ads let people know a company has a job opening. Others may share important public information. They may encourage people to stop smoking or to eat healthful foods. But most ads want to convince a consumer to buy something.

Ads take many different forms. They appear on television, in magazines, and on billboards. Today, a large number of the ads people see are on the Internet. Some ads, such as the banner ads at the top of a Web page, include text and images. Others cover up an entire page while they play their advertising message. Ads may even appear within the games people play online.

ONLINE ADVERTISING

It's important to understand advertising and how it works. The goal of advertisers is to sell products to consumers. Because of this, they place ads wherever

BUYING
ONLINE

Advertisers want to be online because many people shop without ever setting foot in a store. They prefer to shop at the same place where they watch movies, catch up on the news, and play games—on the Internet. In December 2015 the Pew Research Center found that nearly 8 in 10 US adults make online purchases.

WAYS THAT US ADULTS USE TECHNOLOGY TO SHOP

ONLINE — 79%
ON A CELL PHONE — 51%
THROUGH SOCIAL MEDIA LINKS — 15%

HOW OFTEN DO US ADULTS SHOP ONLINE?

- Weekly
- A few times a month
- Less than a few times a month
- Never

28%
37%
20%
15%

IN-GAME
ADVERTISING

Many gamers try to avoid advertising. Chaya Soggot, chief executive of the ad company Woobi, works to ensure that they don't. She recommends companies buy in-game ads because nearly 2 billion gamers play for more than 3 billion hours a week worldwide. That figure includes the 80 percent of smartphone users who play games on their phones. A quarter of these people are younger than 18. Half are 18 to 49, and the rest are older than 49. With this age spread, Soggot says, almost every company can find part of their audience through in-game ads.

people work or play. They run ads wherever people will see them. That's why there are so many ads online.

Digital marketing experts are people whose business is online advertising. They have to know where people are online, what ads get their attention, and what makes them want to buy. In 2015 a group of these experts estimated the average American sees between 4,000 and 10,000 ads every day.

With the number of advertisements surrounding us, every day can feel like a trip through Times Square in New York City.

The truth is that ads are everywhere people look. Ads can accompany e-mail or pop up when people use their smartphones to play a game. People scroll past ads when they visit websites on their tablets. In order to watch a video, a viewer often has to watch an ad first. Because ads are so hard to avoid online, it is important to understand what ads are. People who don't can be tricked into buying things they don't need.

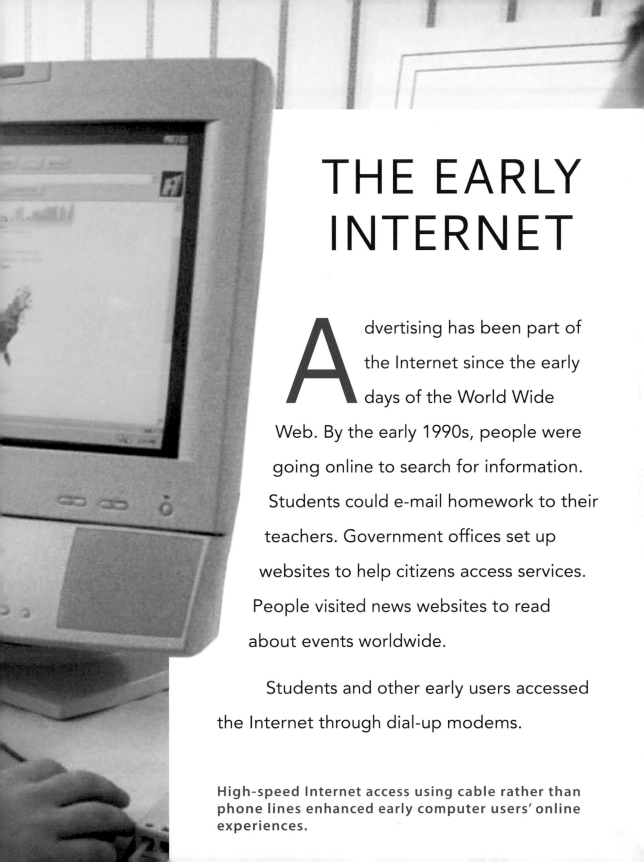

THE EARLY INTERNET

Advertising has been part of the Internet since the early days of the World Wide Web. By the early 1990s, people were going online to search for information. Students could e-mail homework to their teachers. Government offices set up websites to help citizens access services. People visited news websites to read about events worldwide.

Students and other early users accessed the Internet through dial-up modems.

High-speed Internet access using cable rather than phone lines enhanced early computer users' online experiences.

These devices connected their computers to the Internet through phone lines. Compared with today's Internet connections, the service was slow. In the late 1990s and 2000s, faster connections became more widely available. These provided what is known as broadband service.

As more and more people used the Internet, the amount of information online grew. Users paid for Internet connections, but they became used to accessing content online for free. At the same time, companies began spending more money to reach their users. As technology improved, it took more work to build a modern website. Many businesses hired experts to design their sites and write content. They also had to pay a fee to the companies that hosted their websites. To cover these costs, some companies charged

The emergence of smartphones such as the iPhone has allowed people to access the Internet from almost anywhere.

users money to view their content. Others sold advertising.

EARLY ADS

Many of the earliest Internet advertisements were banner ads and pop-up ads. Banner ads span the top or sides of a page. Pop-ups appear in a new window over the website. They block the content that users want to see until the ad is closed. This type of ad irritates many users.

Still, ads paid for content, and Internet

usage grew. Today people use their smartphones, tablets, and laptops to go online. They play games, interact on social media, and do their homework. They read articles and books, listen to music, and watch videos. Sometimes they use the Internet to learn about what is going on in the world. Other times they simply use it to relax.

Online advertising kept pace with the growing importance of the Internet. Businesses find potential customers online. But pop-ups and videos that automatically play

THE FIRST BANNER AD

"Have you ever clicked your mouse right here? You will." Printed in a rainbow font, this was all the first banner ad said. It was created for the telephone company AT&T in 1994. It ran for three months on HotWired, the online version of *Wired* magazine. Forty-four percent of the people who saw this ad clicked through to a landing page with links leading to information on landmarks worldwide. The ad showed people how the Internet, which was still very new, could take them around the world with just a few clicks.

Pop-up ads are one of many annoying features that some computer users want to avoid.

are distracting. They slow down people's devices. They make pages take longer to load.

Consumers searched for a solution to these problems. They wanted to get rid of the ads. When they found ways to do this, advertising companies were forced to adapt.

STRAIGHT TO THE
SOURCE

Scott Cunningham is the founder of the Internet Advertising Bureau Tech Lab, an international organization of advertisers. Cunningham wrote on his blog about issues with online advertising.

We messed up. As technologists tasked with delivering content and services to users, we lost track of the user experience. Twenty years ago we saw an explosion of websites, built by developers around the world, providing all forms of content. This was the beginning of an age of enlightenment, the intersection of content and technology. . . . Digital advertising became the foundation of an economic engine that, still now, sustains the free and democratic World Wide Web. . . . We were so clever and so good at it that we over-engineered the capabilities of the plumbing laid down by, well, ourselves. This steamrolled the users, depleted their devices and tried their patience.

Source: Scott Cunningham. "Getting LEAN with Digital Ad UX." *IAB Tech Lab*. IAB, October 15, 2015. Web. Accessed June 2, 2017.

What's the Big Idea?
Carefully read this excerpt from Cunningham's blog post. What is the main idea? What details does he use to support this idea?

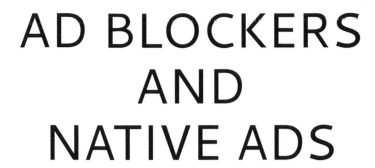

AD BLOCKERS AND NATIVE ADS

To get away from online advertising, people started using programs called ad blockers. These programs use filters to block unwanted content. The filters can recognize common types of online ads. They prevent the ads from loading on the computer. The user simply sees a blank space where the ad would be.

Blocked ads don't get any clicks. No clicks means no money for the website hosting the ads. Companies need the money earned by ads so they can maintain their sites and create

Product placement in movies can be subtle; sometimes it's more obvious.

new content. This is why some websites ask users not to use ad blockers. But people aren't likely to disable their ad blockers on sites that feature annoying ads.

One way for advertisers to get around ad blockers is to blend their ads in with a website's content. This is known as native advertising.

GOING NATIVE

Native advertising has been around for a long time. In the 1980s, native ads called infomercials began

Advertisers can pay to be placed at the top of a list of search engine results.

Wallpaper

Online Deals

1-25 of 4,000,000+ results - Refine Search

One Stop Shop for Online Deals

Hot deals in 2009... You've come to the right place to find
our **online** selection of top quality merchandise...
www.**online-deals**-from-us.com/deals/=4563q45merchandi

Cache

Online Deals that Can't Be Beat

Get the best online **deals** for whatever your budget may be. W
through so you'll be certain to make the best choice possible.
www.class_act_**deals**_today/hot-products/merchande_of_the_s
webproducts_**online**.asp

Cache

Deal Hunter - Find Great Deals Online -Deal-Chaser-today-u

Need help finding that perfect **deal**. You've come to the right place
online deal without any of the fuss that usually comes along with it
ww.deal-chaser-today-usamerica.net/products/bargains_**online**.
che

p Online for Deals

DON'T BE A
BOTHER

Internet users are used to seeing ads. They like some of them. They ignore others. In July 2016, the marketing software company Hubspot asked more than 1,000 Internet users to name which types of advertising they dislike.

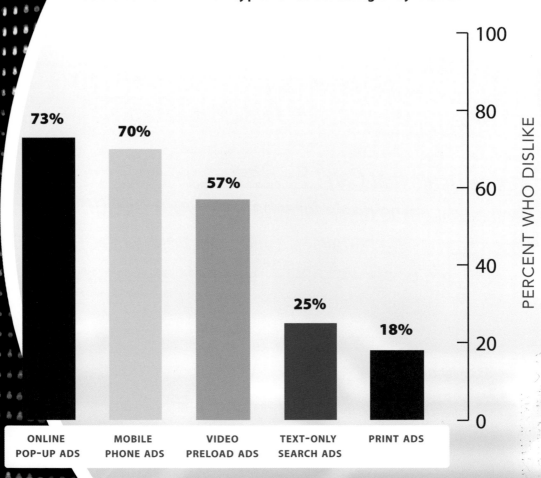

PERCENT WHO DISLIKE

73%	70%	57%	25%	18%
ONLINE POP-UP ADS	MOBILE PHONE ADS	VIDEO PRELOAD ADS	TEXT-ONLY SEARCH ADS	PRINT ADS

It can be difficult to differentiate between advertising and content on some websites.

airing on TV. Infomercials are 30-minute commercials for a single product. These ads demonstrate how to use the product and provide viewers with a phone number to call to purchase it. Some of these products sold in stores still come in boxes labeled "As Seen on TV."

In the 1990s, search ads were among the first online native ads. When someone uses Google or Bing to search for information, these ads top the results page. Companies can buy ads that will appear with specific searches. For example, a user might search for the term *smartphone*. Companies that make smartphones can pay to make sure their ads appear on the results page. The links are identified as ads, but they otherwise appear similar to real search results. Other types of native ads may look like normal posts on social media websites, such as Facebook and Twitter.

Another early native ad was sponsored content. It is undetected by most ad blockers, because it looks like the surrounding content. These articles, images, and videos look like the content people want. For example, a website that features movie news may have a piece of sponsored content about an upcoming movie. It may look like a normal article, but the movie studio paid to have it published.

EXPLORE ONLINE

Chapter Three discusses ad blockers and native advertising. Visit the website listed below and read the definition of native advertising. Examine the examples of what native advertising looks like. What new information did you read in the article? What information did the article contain that is similar to Chapter Three?

WHAT IS NATIVE ADVERTISING?
abdocorelibrary.com/advertising-overload

CHAPTER FOUR

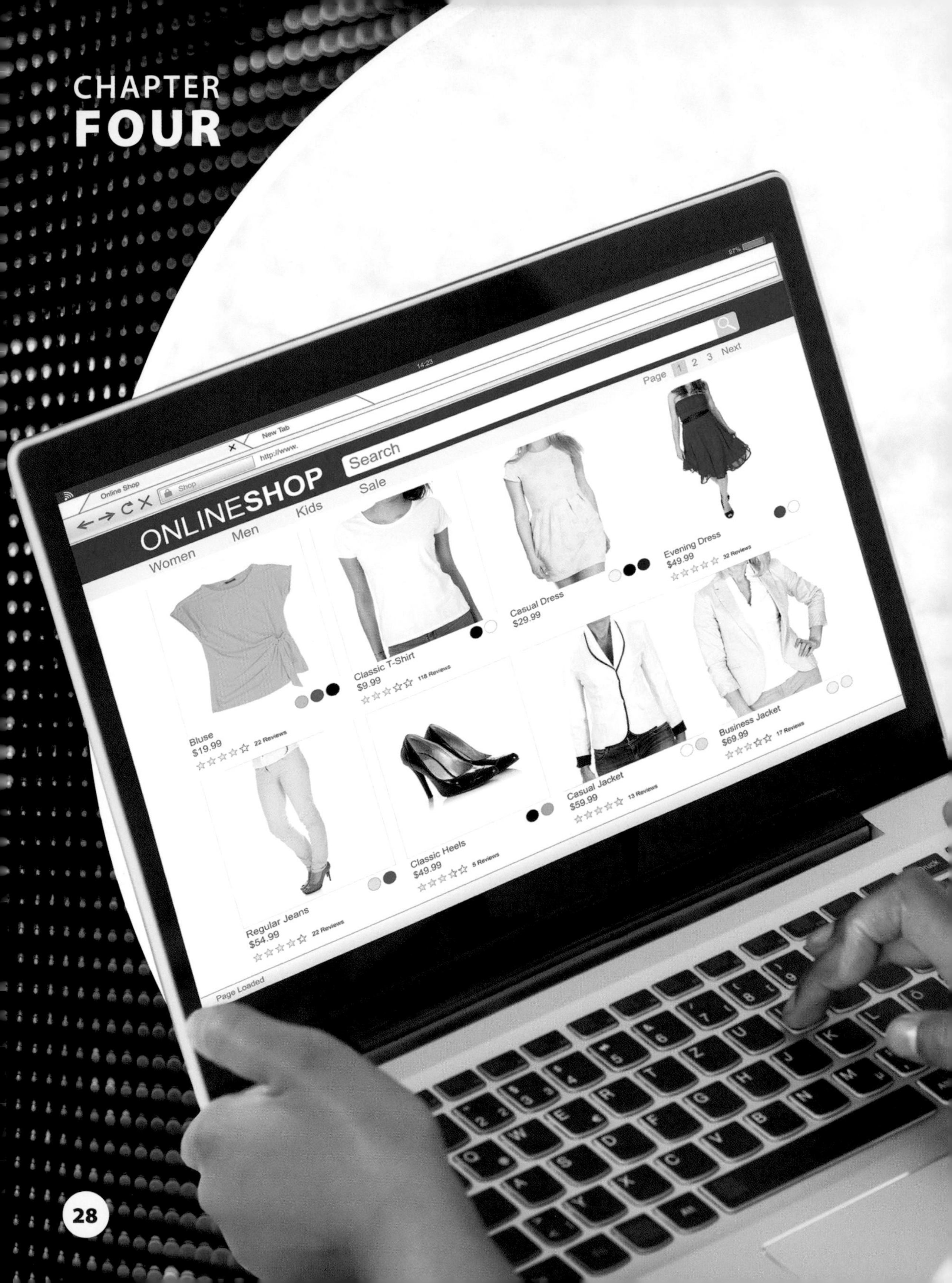

YOUR PERSONAL INFORMATION

In the past, companies had little control over who saw their ads. They paid to show ads to wide audiences and hoped that some viewers would be interested. Today, this has changed. Technology allows companies to target ads at individual people. This makes the job of advertisers easier. But it also means users are giving up their personal information.

For example, imagine a person uses a search engine to look up some shoes she wants to buy. The next time she visits Facebook, she

When you search the Web for products, online retailers can use that information to show you targeted advertising.

PRIVACY AND YOUR PERSONAL INFORMATION

The US Department of Justice (DOJ) has a warning for anyone who uses social media or posts photos online: guard all personal information. Personal information goes beyond what someone buys and her home address, social security number, and full name. It includes where she goes to school and the name of her soccer team. It also includes her Internet history, an important set of data for advertisers. The DOJ encourages online users to guard their information to keep themselves safe.

might see ads for the same shoes. When she goes to a shopping website later, she sees even more ads for the shoes.

This user has been targeted. When she browsed for information earlier, her searches were recorded on her device. The websites she visited knew what she had searched for. They showed her ads based on that information.

This targeting is done using small pieces of data called cookies.

Online retailers such as Amazon track your surfing and shopping habits in an attempt to tailor their advertisements to your interests.

COOKIES—NOT JUST FOR SNACKING

Cookies are text files that are saved on a computer.

The information recorded varies widely. Some cookies

INFO FOR SALE

Advertisers preach the benefits of gathering information to target advertising. This information, saved as a cookie, helps them deliver ads about games to people who play games and ads for music to music fans. Ali Lange, policy analyst for the Center for Democracy and Technology, reminds consumers that Google and Amazon don't just use cookies. They also use Web trackers to see which sites individual users visit, and they sell this information to other companies. Even when people aren't buying something, they may be part of a business transaction. If they aren't shopping, it might be their information for sale.

record user names and passwords. This makes it easier to log in to commonly used sites. Other cookies record a user's searches, such as for a specific pair of shoes.

When one site accesses a cookie created by another site, it can use the information. This is why if a person looks for shoes on a sporting goods website, an ad for the same sporting goods website will later appear elsewhere. The ad has been targeted to match something this person is interested in.

The ad could also be for the same shoe that the person looked for on the sporting goods site. Or it might be an ad for sports shoes in general. If the user is a gamer, the ad might be for games similar to ones the user has already bought. Advertisers believe that users are more likely to click on a targeted ad. They prefer showing ads to customers they already know are interested in them.

FURTHER EVIDENCE

Chapter Four covers cookies and how advertisers use the information they provide. Go to the website below and explore the ideas that you find there about cookies and how they work. Find a quote from the site that supports the chapter's discussion of cookies.

HOW DO ADVERTISERS SHOW ME CUSTOM ADS?
abdocorelibrary.com/advertising-overload

UNITED

FE
TR
CO
BU

WHAT'S ACCEPTABLE?

Advertising is part of the Internet. It is necessary to pay for the costs of building and running a website. Without all of this, running today's Internet would not be possible. However, online ads are unpopular when they get in the way of what people want to do online. Native ads instead seek to blend in with websites. Sometimes this can provide people with information that interests them. But it can also disguise itself as regular content. It may not look like an ad. How can consumers tell the difference?

The Federal Trade Commission offices are housed with other government agencies in Washington, DC.

BUY IT

Many experts believe that meaningful native content is something most companies can achieve. Simon Dumenco, a columnist for *Advertising Age*, disagrees. He believes it's difficult to make advertising content feel important to consumers. Some ads are funny and will be shared with others. But many other ads are ignored. Dumenco thinks that many companies find it impossible to tell an interesting story again and again, because their only message is "buy me." Because of this, he says, the Internet will be flooded with boring and annoying native ads.

TRANSPARENT AND MEANINGFUL

The Federal Trade Commission (FTC) is a government department. It protects consumers from unfair business practices, including unfair ads. The FTC says that people need to know when they are looking at an ad.

Sometimes this means the ad must be labeled. This is the case when an ad looks like a search result. Those that appear at the top of a Google search are labeled "Ad." Ads that look like simple Twitter posts also have to be clearly marked. Twitter uses the label "Promoted."

Content that needs to be labeled will vary from site to site. If an ad for art supplies appears on a site that focuses on drawing, the ad might need to be labeled. Ads that use borders or unique lettering to clearly stand out from the rest of the content may not need to be labeled. But they often are labeled just to be clear that they're ads.

YOUTUBE ADS

YouTube can be a tricky place for young Internet users to navigate. Is that an informational video about virtual reality goggles? Or is it an ad? It depends on who is paying for it. YouTuber Austin Evans was on set to watch the filming of ads for the oil company Castrol. The ads involved virtual reality gear. Evans told his viewers about the exciting experience, showing them the virtual reality gear. But at the beginning of the video Evans tells viewers, "Castrol EDGE Motor Oil invited me out to the set of their latest project." That statement indicates that the video is a sponsored ad.

Almost all social media platforms contain advertising, but some do a better job of blending the ads into the rest of the content.

If the same drawing site had an ad for athletic shoes, it might not need to label the ad. Users are less likely to think it's content from the website.

But clearly defined ads aren't enough. People also want meaningful content that helps them in some way. A marketing study by the company Edelman Berland was released in 2014. It showed that 60 percent of news consumers don't mind native advertising if it tells a story, informs, or entertains rather than just promoting a product.

For example, consumers may not care who wrote a piece on rock climbing as long as it tells them something new about the sport. A link at the end of the video that would send them to a sporting goods store may be deemed acceptable if the video is fun and informative. Exciting photos of a young climber hanging off a cliff might be sponsored by the company that made his shoes. That's okay with some consumers. The photos are still interesting. The information is useful. For many users, content matters the most, not who created it. They just don't want to be tricked.

STRAIGHT TO THE
SOURCE

The FTC wrote a set of guidelines that cover native advertising. Here is one example of a type of ad that violates the guidelines:

> A game app tests players' skills to survive in the wilderness and offers a choice of supplies and equipment in each game phase. When players tap to make a choice, a box appears containing a selection of items—for example, a flashlight, a rope, and a hatchet. . . Among the items players can select is a bar of soap identified by brand name with the text "Clean up." If tapped, the soap icon takes the player out of the game and into the soap manufacturer's branded game app. Based on consumers' customary use of the game and the similarity of the soap to other items players can select in the game, consumers might not recognize the icon as an ad before tapping and leaving the game.
>
> Source: "Native Advertising: A Guide for Businesses." *Federal Trade Commission*. FTC, December 2015. Web. Accessed May 4, 2017.

Consider Your Audience

How would you rewrite this to help a young gamer understand what a native ad looks like and how it should be labeled?

FAST FACTS

- The earliest Internet ads were banner ads and pop-ups. Paid advertising, like these early ads and more recent native ads, allows Internet content to be free to consumers.

- Native ads are ads that blend in with the surrounding content. They make it harder to identify advertising on a website.

- Targeted ads use personal information to identify consumers who might be interested in what the ad is promoting.

- The Federal Trade Commission (FTC) requires that ads be "clear and transparent." This means that people need to know they are looking at an ad. To achieve this, ads should be labeled "ad," "advertisement," "sponsored content," or "paid content." Some content uses other terminology to indicate it's an ad. If the author of an article or the star of a video says he was "invited" to see something special, it's likely an ad for that product.

STOP AND
THINK

Say What?

Reading about advertising means learning a lot of new vocabulary. Find five words in this book that you had never heard before. Use a dictionary to find what these words mean. Next, write the meanings in your own words. Finally, use each word in a new sentence.

Dig Deeper

After reading this book, what questions do you still have about online advertising in general or native advertising in particular? With an adult's help, find a few reliable sources that can help you answer your questions. Write a paragraph about what you learned.

Surprise Me

Chapter Three discusses how native ads blend in so people don't realize they are looking at an ad. After reading this book, what two or three facts about native ads did you find most surprising? Write a few sentences about each fact. Why did you find each fact surprising?

GLOSSARY

ad blocker
a computer program that blocks advertisements on websites

banner ad
an ad that spans the top of a Web page

consumers
people who buy, or consume, products such as clothing, games, videos, or food

cookies
text files used to store information such as a user name and password or to track a user's Web history

host
to store a website's data so it can be accessed online

native advertising
advertising that blends in with the surrounding content

pop-up ad
an ad that opens a new window that must be closed to view the main Web page

sponsor
a company that provides funds as part of a continued relationship

targeted
selected or chosen

transparent
without a hidden agenda or purpose

ONLINE RESOURCES

To learn more about online advertising, visit our free resource websites below.

Visit **abdocorelibrary.com** for free Common Core resources for teachers and students, including vetted activities, multimedia, and booklinks, for deeper subject comprehension.

Visit **abdobooklinks.com** for free additional online weblinks for further learning. These links are routinely monitored and updated to provide the most current information available.

LEARN MORE

Graydon, Shari. *Made You Look: How Advertising Works and Why You Should Know.* Toronto, Ontario, Canada: Annick Press, 2013.

Harris, Duchess, and Elizabeth Herschbach. *Your Personalized Internet.* Minneapolis, MN: Abdo Publishing, 2018.

ABOUT THE
AUTHORS

Duchess Harris, JD, PhD

Professor Harris is the chair of the American Studies Department at Macalester College. The author and coauthor of four books (*Hidden Human Computers: The Black Women of NASA* and *Black Lives Matter* with Sue Bradford Edwards, *Racially Writing the Republic: Racists, Race Rebels, and Transformations of American Identity* with Bruce Baum, and *Black Feminist Politics from Kennedy to Clinton/Obama*), she has been an associate editor for *Litigation News*, the American Bar Association Section's quarterly flagship publication, and was the first editor-in-chief of *Law Raza Journal*, an interactive online race and the law journal for William Mitchell College of Law.

She has earned a PhD in American Studies from the University of Minnesota and a Juris Doctorate from William Mitchell College of Law.

Sue Bradford Edwards

Sue Bradford Edwards is a Missouri nonfiction author who writes about science, culture, and history. Her other books include *Hidden Human Computers: The Black Women of NASA* and *Black Lives Matter*, both with Duchess Harris.

INDEX